BLACK
TO THE
FUTURE

Lessons from Black Wall Street for
Community and Economic Prosperity

LaRachelle Samuel-Smith, PhD
and William H. Turner, PhD

PAGE PUBLISHING
Conneaut Lake, PA

First originally published by Page Publishing 2024

ISBN 979-8-89315-044-5 (pbk)
ISBN 979-8-89315-064-3 (digital)

Printed in the United States of America

INTRODUCTION

Between its noble ideals regarding equality and tormented realities with race matters, life in America has presented significant challenges across several domains. As we are more than twenty years past the dawn of the twenty-first century, a cursory view of the current economic state of Black America paints a relatively positive picture, progress, as it were. Yet a deeper inspection into the realities reveals a different picture, ripe with gross inequities. Even as the past fifty years reveal significant improvements for Black people in areas such as politics (the election of Barack Obama as president), education (affirmative action in college admissions), and sports and entertainment, for example, the struggle for equality is far from over. The factors that contribute to these disparities are multi-faceted, resulting in adverse outcomes that are far-reaching for people of color in America, particularly for Black Americans.

According to data and analyses reported in *The Economic State of Black America in 2020* by the Joint

*LaRachelle Samuel-Smith, PhD
and William H. Turner, PhD*

Economic Committee,[1] Black Americans, as a group, continue to fare far worse than Whites, as evidenced by the statistics below:

- *Income.* "The gap between Black and White annual household incomes is about $29,000 per year." This is partly because Black workers earn only fifty-nine cents to every dollar a White person earns.
- *Poverty.* "Black Americans are over twice as likely to live in poverty as White Americans."
- *Wealth.* Black wealth equals less than one-tenth that of White wealth: $17,000 and $171,000, respectively.
- *Homeownership.* Black families have lower rates of homeownership than White families, 42 percent for Blacks and 73 percent for Whites.
- *Life expectancy.* Life expectancy for non-Hispanic Black Americans is 3.6 years lower than for non-Hispanic White Americans
- *Unemployment.* Black rates of unemployment have historically been about double the rate of Whites. In 2020, the rates were 6.0 percent for Blacks and 3.1 percent for Whites.

These factors are interrelated and the dynamics of Blacks as entrepreneurs and business owners are crucial to the overall economic health of neighborhoods in America's cities where Blacks are concentrated. Particularly regarding Black wealth, the outstanding "wealth gap" that exists is directly tied to historical practices of exclusion and the de facto and de jure-sanctioned destruction of sources of Black wealth. Though not our focus here, the debate around reparations is framed inside what Swedish sociologist Gunnar Myrdal called *The American Dilemma*, the title of his highly-regarded book, published in 1944.

The survival of the Black community is a testament to the perseverance, resilience, and spirit and determination of Blacks, going back to the beginning of their enslavement. Of course, much is known about the stories of White industry tycoons such as Andrew Carnegie, J. P. Morgan, and John D Rockefeller. But little is celebrated about (their) Black business counterparts—trailblazers such as O. W. Gurley, J. B. Stradford, Madame C. J. Walker, and A. J. Smitherman. These lesser-known individuals were thought leaders more than a century ago, and their stories can teach us today about community and economic development.

The Legacy of Black Wall Street

At the turn of the twentieth century, America came into its own as a global economic power; this status was a direct result of more than three centuries as the world's dominant slave broker. Yet at the time, Black Americans were but one generation removed from the realities of slavery, and then they were thrust into the subjugation of Jim Crow and continued practices of race-based terrorism (e.g., lynchings).

During the Reconstruction Era (1863–1877) and into the early 1900s, many all-Black towns began to emerge. One such settlement was created in Tulsa, Oklahoma, a cohesive community known as Greenwood. Due to Greenwood's economic success—as evidenced by the proliferation of Black-owned businesses that lined the town's main street along Greenwood Avenue—the town became known as Black Wall Street. The account of the people's achievements is not only remarkable because of what they were able to accomplish, but it is invaluable for its lessons that are still applicable today. In the following pages, we will demonstrate what this enduring legacy can teach us about business and community and how to harness this knowledge to advance Black entrepreneurship in the twenty-first century and beyond.

Greenwood District

Greenwood was borne of several factors that converged simultaneously, but it was foremost the intentional synergy between like-minded Black entrepreneurs of the day. Although de jure and de facto segregation played a role in setting and maintaining the boundaries of its residents, early Black businessmen who settled this burgeoning oil-sourced town had a shared vision to create a self-sustaining all-Black enclave that would facilitate the progress of the race.[2] To that end, they erected "luxury shops, restaurants, grocery stores, hotels, jewelry and clothing stores, movie theaters, barbershops and salons, a library, pool halls, nightclubs and offices for doctors, lawyers and dentists" as well as a "school system, post office, a savings and loan bank, hospital, and bus and taxi service."

The Greenwood District of Tulsa, over thirty-five city blocks, created the conditions for its residents to control an "active cultural, political, and social life."[3] As the population in greater Tulsa increased, so did the population of Greenwood. With the district's emphasis on self-governance and self-sufficiency, a "for Black, by Black" ("For Us, By Us" or FUBU) brand and philosophy, Greenwood became known as a community in which Black people could seek refuge from "economic, social, and political oppression."[4] As more Black entrepreneurs were attracted to the area, the district flourished. Local businesses patronized each other's services, and it is estimated that every dollar circulated—within the Black community—at least thirty times, propelling a critical mass of Greenwood Blacks not only to unprecedented wealth but unparalleled independence from White control, a phenomenon that ran counter to American history, particularly in the South.

LaRachelle Samuel-Smith, PhD
and William H. Turner, PhD

Architects of Prosperity

Although it was the foresight of different businesspeople that conceived the idea of Greenwood and took the steps that initiated its inception, it must be noted that the vision could not have been realized without community support. With that said, we would like to focus on a few of the pioneers of Greenwood's Black business community and show briefly how they were deliberate and calculating and strategic about providing opportunities for Black people to succeed despite the harsh realities of life during this era of the sanctioned subjugation of Black people in America and throughout the African diaspora as well.

O. W. Gurley

A principal designer of the Greenwood neighborhood, O. W. Gurley moved to Oklahoma with his wife in the early 1890s, originally settling in a town called Perry. In Perry, he became a prominent community member and a wealthy businessman. However, his enterprising spirit continued to fuel his passion for a better life for all Black people. This drive led him to move to Tulsa in 1905, where he purchased over forty acres of land, the vehicle he used to empower other Black people. His plan involved dividing his land into residential and commercial plots with the policy of selling only to Black people. Here, he built the first businesses in the town, including a boarding house and a grocery store; this was the beginning of Greenwood.

J. B. Stradford

A law school graduate, J. B. Stradford was a successful businessman in Kentucky before coming to Tulsa. He, like Gurley, had a vision of creating a prosperous all-Black community, driven by his belief that Black people should pool their resources for economic progress. When Stradford came to Tulsa in 1898, he began to map out his idea, and when Gurley arrived in the early 1900s, together, they started planning what would later become Greenwood. For his part, Stradford, a former hotel owner, erected a fifty-five-room luxury hotel—the largest Black-owned hotel in the nation at the time—as one of the crown jewels of the district.

A. J. Smitherman

A. J. Smitherman was also a key figure in the development of the Greenwood business district. He came to Indian Territory in the 1890s with his family. His vital contribution to the community was the establishment of one of the town's two newspapers, *The Tulsa Star*. This communication vehicle enlightened residents about essential news and legal issues of concern to Black people, helping to forge a cohesive and informed populace.

Pillars of Success

The three entrepreneurs (and countless others), in conjunction with the community, achieved economic success through the implementation of six core principles: (1) access to resources, (2) collaboration, (3) education, (4) health care, (5) communication, and (6) ownership. These pillars form the framework for executing best practices for vibrant communities and effective businesses.

Those mainstay values and goals are analyzed in this text with regard to their importance to spatially identifiable Black communities and entrepreneurship as applied to the uniqueness of Black Wall Street, and how these apply to the present-day Black communities and economic empowerment.

CHAPTER 1

Access to Resources

When we consider the role that access to resources plays in the economic development of communities, an initial step is to illuminate the diverse types of resources, particularly, as it relates to the economic status of Black Americans. It is also necessary to delve into *barriers* erected against Blacks to access resources (such as bank loans and government programs) and the effect of these official impediments on the creation of Black wealth.

Access to Resources: The Importance to
Business and Community Development

A *resource* is "a supply of something that a country, an organization or a person has and can use,

1

especially to increase their wealth."[5] This definition informs us of two key points: (1) a resource can be used to increase wealth, and (2) (a) resource(s) must be accessed for capital and wealth to be actualized and realized.

Historically, Black Americans have struggled to access financial resources for the betterment of themselves and their communities; whether in the form of capital, credit, information, or connections. This situation has created unfavorable outcomes resulting in a depressed effect on individuals, communities, and the economy of Black communities as a whole. Specifically for Black Americans, this lack of access has been a significant barrier to wealth-building, contributing to the considerable wealth gap between White and Black Americans.

When the economy and business exchanges of a community are controlled by persons *outside* that community, those persons then *control* the education of that community, the health care in that community, the politics of that community, the housing and real estate in that community: the virtual totality of that community. Logically, a "wealth gap" will remain between those *in* the community (consumers) and those outside that community (those who *own* and *conduct* and *control* the economy of that community.

The controllers get richer and richer and the consumers get poorer and poorer.

The wealth gap is "the product of complex interactions among social, historical, political, and institutional forces," some of which are revealed in the obstacles below:[6]

- Due to housing discrimination, Black people have been locked into specific neighborhoods and locked out of others.
- Policies enacted under initiatives such as the New Deal and the GI Bill, which facilitated the "asset creation of an American middle class," were exclusionary to Blacks and favorable to Whites.[7]
- Because Black individuals do not often receive inheritances, their "starter" wealth is much lower than White individuals.
- Upon college completion, many Black graduates face financial burdens related to supporting parents or increased student debt compared to White college graduates.
- Barriers to accessing credit for Black people continue to be a reality, as a recent study revealed the inequitable distribution of

PPP loans and increased adverse treatment of Black applicants.[8]

- In the employment arena, Black people can often be excluded from the information networks that are requisites for advancement and awareness of opportunities.

The examples above are only a fraction of the disadvantages experienced by Black people, which are precipitated, in large measure, by the barriers to Blacks' access to resources. This rejection of Blacks' access to resources negatively impacts their ability to generate wealth, limiting individual (and the group's) ability to progress economically. However, when conditions such as what existed in the Greenwood District before the pogrom are favorable, Black individuals, Black-owned businesses, and the Black community prosper. Ideally, a rising tide raises all boats.

Black Wall Street: Model for Success

A tool that was central to how the residents of Black Wall Street were able to thrive was the mindset of its founders, which placed a premium on *intentionally* securing, promoting, and sharing access to resources solely for Black people. Although everyone

in Greenwood was not rich, the citizens all partici-
pated in the orderliness of the economic system that
was created by the persons and the practices that they
themselves founded and facilitated which created
community-based wealth, ultimately benefiting this
Black neighborhood in Oklahoma's second largest
city.

O. W. Gurley and J. B. Stradford, the two key
developers of the Greenwood District, had a similar
vision fueled by a desire to advance the Black race. To
that end, they allowed their passions to propel their
dreams into reality. Stradford believed that economic
progress for Black people depended on the pooling
of resources. Gurley's foresight regarding migration
led him to buy land, portion it for sale, and offer his
lots to Blacks only. This initial access to property for
Black people was a monumental resource in and of
itself. However, as Greenwood expanded, there were
several practices relative to access to resources that
forged its growing success, including the following:

- Gurley established a system that provided
  loans for other entrepreneurs that wanted to
  start businesses. He also created an employment agency to help migrant workers.

- The residents' income circulated within the community for extended periods. Even those who worked outside of Greenwood spent their money within the district. Also, some business owners in Greenwood, such as Simon Berry and Gurley, made business connections with entities in the greater Tulsa area. Again, their gains also filtered into Greenwood's economy, enriching the overall community.

- Instituting two newspapers, *The Tulsa Star* and the *Oklahoma Sun*, was a glorious accomplishment for a people who were formerly unable to learn to read by law and served as a critical vehicle for disseminating information, of which oppressors had for so long tried to deprive Black people.

- Businesses within the district supported one another. For example, the Acme Brick Company supplied businesses with the bricks needed to build their buildings.

Best Practices: Connecting the Past and the Present

According to a present-day descendant of Black Wall Street, John W. Rogers, Jr., "Greenwood shows that when we are left to our own devices and don't have a knee to our neck, we can achieve extraordinary things." Having a mindset that prioritizes community and ensuring access to resources is a winning combination towards reaching that goal. Here are some best practices for business owners to implement.

- *Business incubators.* Developing spaces where Black entrepreneurs can access loans, business, and employment opportunities and an information network to provide services such as mentoring and access to investors. Utilizing strategies specifically designed to address common barriers faced by Black business owners is crucial.
- *Mutual support networks.* Creating systems where businesses support one another through cross-use of services and pooling of resources.

CHAPTER 2

Collaboration

Community denotes identifying with a particular group. Residents of a specific community often have shared values and work together to achieve common goals. This notion of working together, or collaboration, is essential to the success of communities, particularly in economic development. *Collaboration*—which is synonymous with *teamwork, partnership, association, alliance,* and *group effort*—is not only an action but also an attitude, a mindset, that fosters collective progress.

*Collaboration: The Importance to Business
and Community Development*

Black people in the United States have a long history of working together to better the community. In the days of enslavement, Black families were deliberately destroyed, but Black people found ways to create cohesive ties to ensure the perpetuation of future generations. This persistent attitude helped Black people as a group to remain focused even in the face of persistent renunciations, repudiations, and rejections of their equality with Whites, to their very humanity.

Black Wall Street: Model for Success

From the start, Greenwood's inception was built on the principle of collaboration. Its two principal founders, O. W. Gurley and J. B. Stradford, worked together to establish the town's purpose and systems that would define its practices, such as selling land to Black people only and making loans to budding entrepreneurs. Both men believed that Greenwood should be a place where Black people could live with dignity and safety. Developing a self-contained structure where its residents had full participation was the solution to produce this ideal.

The people's participation was essential because the model was not based on an unsustainable one-way "handout" or "trickle-down economics." But both these founders and the people at large had a *shared responsibility* in making the community a success. This meant that the people had to buy into the benefits of collaboration, and the entrepreneurs had to believe in the value of investing in the community.

One of the dynamic features of the community was how—and how long—the residents' dollars circulated within their neighborhood before leaving. This undoubtedly enriched the lives of all the community members as it allowed businesses to grow and wealth to increase exponentially. Another key application was how businesses supported one another. This practice also was responsible for developing the economy of the neighborhood.

Best Practices: Connecting the Past and the Present

While the adage "With great wealth comes great responsibility" is attributed to uber-wealthy businessman and philanthropist, Bill Gates, it is from the Christian Bible, Luke 12:48, that one finds the timeless reference to this quotation: "For everyone to whom much is given, from him much will be required."[9] These two quotes share a similar sentiment: individuals are responsible for being wise custodians of their resources, including financial resources. This concept highlights the primary basis for the first of the three practices below, namely that established Black entrepreneurs bear responsibility for investing in the economic success of the Black community.

- *Investment.* Those desiring to enter into business must be taught that creating wealth takes time. Those established business owners with a heart for the community have a duty to invest in the community with time, talent, and resources.
- *Mindset and education.* Greenwood was a place, but it was also a mindset, a spirit; it begins with this. The revitalization of communities starts with the revitalization of minds. Entrepreneurs must be in the business of education that heralds the how-tos and benefits of elements such as money management and the positive impact of collaboration on the economy.
- *Mutual support networks.* Already mentioned in chapter 1, these structures must also support intracollaboration where diverse voices are amplified.

CHAPTER 3

Education

Formal education was a pursuit that was historically denied to Black Americans. Despite this, or perhaps because of it, educational attainment remains a high value among Black Americans. From learning to read in secret to integrating public schools, establishing HBCUs, and graduating from Ivy League institutions, Black people have forged paths in education that have surpassed their ancestors' wildest imaginings. Yet in the twenty-first century, the data shows that the promising achievements of Blacks in (higher) education have not translated into overall progress. Despite the economic benefits of college attendance and graduation, there are noteworthy inequities in the employment status and overall income outcomes of college graduates when controlled by racial and ethnic metrics. No matter the level of educational attainment, Whites have higher income levels than Blacks (workers).

Education: The Importance to Business and Community Development

Most have heard the saying "Knowledge is power." This is true, but knowledge is not the lone pathway to success.

It is a well-known fact that Black people attain higher levels of formal education (proportionately) than Whites from comparable economic backgrounds. Nevertheless, this ironic fact does not lead (proportionately) to increased wealth for Black people. While education is a wise investment, educational attainment, as a lone factor, for Blacks at least is often a source of indebtedness (i.e., repaying exorbitant student loans). Significant amounts of inherited money (the *intergenerational* transfer of wealth) remain a "white privilege."

Black Wall Street: Model for Success

From the Greenwood community, scores of oral histories and autobiographies reflect on the importance of "educating the next generation." The "colored section of Tulsa" operated a school system, including Booker T. Washington High School, which challenged its students with a rigorous curriculum of both college prep and trade-oriented courses. Because of this emphasis, teachers were compensated commensurate to the value placed on education and were some of the highest-paid workers in the district. However, supporting budding businesspersons was also an integral part of the informal instruction and moral compass that guided those who walked and worked along Black Wall Street. The priority placed on formal education and the acquisition of trades in Greenwood which symbolized and emphasized the mentorship of new Black entrepreneurs and skilled workers embodies the inventiveness and resourcefulness that can serve the interests of Blacks presently and into the future. While the Akan (Ghana / West Africa) word *Sankofa* was not used by the builders of the Greenwood District, its meaning—"It is not taboo to fetch what is at risk of being left behind"—is quite much in vogue among Black millennials.

Best Practices: Connecting the Past and the Present

Formal education is a worthwhile pursuit—an undertaking that opens doors and creates access to opportunities (and people) that might otherwise be inaccessible. However, in addition to Blacks obtaining academic credentials and certification in the skilled crafts, modern-day Black businesses people—those of the ilk and attitude of Greenwood's founding fathers—must devise and advocate for and instruct novices in strategies that support the growth of inter-generational wealth that not only enriches individuals but strengthens Black communities as well.

Like the entrepreneurs of Black Wall Street who purchased land in preparation for a future that had yet to materialize, Black businesses today need to have an eye toward the future, particularly as it relates to finding ways to capture the enormous and growing spending power of Black Americans, which represents about a trillion dollars a year.[10] Black companies must not only have this as a goal but they must lead the charge in creatively pursuing this market and teach others to do the same. Additionally, businesses must be champions of instruction in general business practices such as how to start a business, access

LaRachelle Samuel-Smith, PhD
and William H. Turner, PhD

capital, and develop systems for passing on economic principles to the youth.[11] We are not unmindful of the impact of gentrification in (formally) Black "districts," such as Harlem in NYC and Houston's four historically Black communities—Fifth and Third Wards and Independence Heights and Sunnyside.

CHAPTER 4

Health Care

People with poor health are less likely to achieve their personal goals and aspirations. Scaled up to the societal level, healthy people not only survive longer than unhealthy ones, but they are more likely to thrive. Overall, the quality of life for most Black Americans is directly correlated to their health standing which is, by and large, significantly inferior, as compared to that of the general population.

Black people experience several unfavorable health measures, such as lower life expectancy rates and higher infant and pregnancy-related mortality rates. Discrimination and lack of access to resources are significant contributors to poor health outcomes. Also, 65 percent of the Black population is concentrated in sixteen states that score below the national average for health care access and quality. And some of the worst health outcomes are associated with a lack of health insurance. "Research has shown that going without health insurance negatively impacts the timing and quality of health care treatment, as well as long-term health outcomes. This, in turn, can substantially reduce financial security, wealth, retirement readiness and other aspects of economic well-being."

*Health Care: The Importance to Business
and Community Development*

Human capital is *the* central driving force that powers business success. Diminished health results in decreased productivity, absenteeism, and ultimately, unrealized and lost revenue. In turn, these adverse consequences lead to repressed economic growth. On the other hand, healthy workplaces have employees with higher job performance and improved morale. These positive consequences amount to an overall improvement in companies' bottom lines and a boost to local economies.

Hospitals, specifically, have a unique position in communities.[12] As principal employers and large-scale purchasers of goods and services, these income-generating institutions are poised to be catalysts for "community revitalization," especially since their "missions and bottom lines...tie them to their respective communities." Institutions focused on community-building contribute to increased health care access for residents and enable people to afford insurance to engage with the services they need. Hospitals' ability to build community wealth also benefits residents by helping them to be able to pay for health care services.

Black Wall Street: Model for Success

Among its many businesses that supplied goods and services to the people of Greenwood was its own hospital. This facility provided jobs for the residents and access to health care, and it was also a source of community building and wealth generation. Like the other staples that constituted the backbone of Greenwood's economy, its hospital supported its people in the spirit of community that epitomized Black Wall Street, allowing for a healthy citizenry fully able to participate in society.

LaRachelle Samuel-Smith, PhD
and William H. Turner, PhD

Best Practices: Connecting the Past and the Present

Although establishing avenues for health care access was imperative for Black people in the early twentieth century (and still is today), the significance of the community incorporating a hospital in Greenwood was greater than erecting a facility for treating Black people affected by discrimination. Their inclusion of an institution that simultaneously fulfilled this need for health care access as well as for a vehicle for community building and wealth creation is a relevant model for today. Businesses can further contribute to this effort by addressing the following aspects:

- *Health care spending.* By investing in health care, Black businesses can support their workers and reap the benefits mentioned above while facilitating economic growth.
- *Workplace health programs.* Institute workplace health programs to support employees in achieving optimal health.
- *Community collaboration.* Work to address health disparities by leveraging the position of local hospitals.

CHAPTER 5

Communication

From the Reconstruction Era into the early twentieth century in America, Black Americans continued to be confronted with many struggles, including discrimination, segregation, and violence. Yet even as these challenges persisted, many Black people, ever-yearning and working for progress and dignified existence, seized upon education and the furtherance of civil rights as vehicles to accomplish their goals.

During this time, communication channels were exploding with inventions like the telegraph and the telephone that allowed for the expansion of information exchange in the larger society and business arena. Another communication innovation that had long since been invented, the printing press, facilitated the birth of the newspaper, enabling communication to mass audiences.

At the end of the Reconstruction Era, Black people became free from the bonds of enslavement and began migrating north and west from the Black Belt South and establishing numerous all-Black towns in the Southwest, communication networks sprouted up, anchored by the establishment of Black newspapers. These precursors to digital telecommunications (periodicals) often became central to community life and development, informing Black citizens and helping them forge a path forward.

*Communication: The Importance to
Business and Community Development*

When we think of advances in communication, such as modern cell phones and the Internet, the humble newspaper of old may seem like a useless relic. Yet these vehicles have similar purposes as "the economy's engine for change and its gateway to resources and opportunities."[13] Furthermore, communication is vital to developing healthy businesses and communities because it "connects key players in the economy, promotes their dialogue, and informs their policies." And for members of underrepresented groups, communication is a means of expression and empowerment.

Black Wall Street: Model for Success

As important as this catalyst for change was, and is, in the larger society, it was an even more significant force for Black communities, including those on Black Wall Street.

Concerning the communication mechanisms employed in Greenwood, they published two newspapers, the premier publication being the *Tulsa Star*, operated by A. J. Smitherman.[14] The paper gave voice to the people's concerns, reporting on topics of interest—many of which major papers would not cover—from a Black perspective. Highlighting Black causes and prominent issues of social change such as voting rights, housing, and education, the *Star* "provided leadership and influence in shaping the community."

Best Practices: Connecting the Past and the Present

Although the days of the newspaper as king are long gone, their value as a communication medium that brought (Black) communities together and spurred economic activity is a model for business success that has been adapted to today's market. Particularly, in this current age of digital communication, businesses must understand and be able to tap into the power of Black influence.[15] This means that Black businesses must have a vibrant online presence and be acutely aware of trends. One such example, *MelaninPeople*, is "the #1 social media platform designed by Black and Brown people for Black people and people of color throughout the world. using short-form videos, pictures, E-magazine, marketplace (commerce) and messaging application." Segmented Marketing Services (Winston-Salem, North Carolina) has been in the business of targeting Blacks for major consumer-product manufacturers for forty years.

It may seem evident that implementing a consumer-focused marketing strategy is prudent, but for this to occur, one must know the demographics of their audience. This is one reason the newspaper in Greenwood was able to aid in the community's success; it was familiar with the people's values and aligned with those values. By keenly honing in on Black influence and the channels of operation, companies can develop products and services that benefit communities and are also profitable.

CHAPTER 6

Ownership

When individuals and businesses stake an ownership claim in communities, they have a vested interest in the welfare of those communities and can contribute to their progress or decline. Unfortunately, for Black Americans, entrenched racism and discrimination have largely excluded them from participation in systems of ownership.

*Ownership: The Importance to Business
and Community Development*

Land ownership and homeownership have long been avenues for wealth creation – at least for whites in America. Wealth generation in America is "as American as cherry pie." In 2020, the US Small

LaRachelle Samuel-Smith, PhD
and William H. Turner, PhD

Business Administration listed 32.5 million small businesses in the US, which accounted for *99.9 percent* of all US businesses. A small business is a firm that has fewer than five hundred employees. Thus, considerable wealth is built via small businesses. Even though Black people have been systematically disenfranchised from the wealth-building potential of small business ownership, when they do manage to "hang the shingle," especially in a Black neighborhood, consumers who live outside that community are not likely to "cross over" into that community to shop for the products and services offered for sale and fees.

With agency over their own businesses, which keeps and recirculates money within Black neighborhoods, and provides the model of leadership, Black ownership facilitates the stability of Black communities. Additionally, when Black-owned businesses are operating in a Black community, they offer "segmented" and customized goods (foodstuffs) and services (beauty and barber shops that meet the exclusive and specialized needs of Black, as well as, other people (ethnic groups), while providing employment opportunities which, in circular fashion, keeps and recirculates the community's dollars within the community.

Black Wall Street: Model for Success

A fundamental characteristic that allowed Black Wall Street to stand so tall was the resilience and doggedness expressed in the dedication and capacity of Black ownership. O. W. Gurley purchased his land in Tulsa as a result of the Dawes Act of 1887, which allotted land in Indian territory to the Black people who were former slaves of Indian tribes (e.g., the Eastern Band of the Cherokee Nation). From that seed, over 150 Black-owned businesses sprouted in Greenwood within twenty years.

In addition to the business owners previously mentioned, among Black Wall Street's enterprising citizens were the following entrepreneurs:[16]

- *John and Loula Williams.* This couple owned and operated several businesses, including an auto repair shop, a confectionary, a rooming house, and the 750-seat Dreamland Theater.
- *Simon Berry.* Mr. Berry owned and operated a car service, a hotel, and an airline charter service.

- *Mary Elizabeth Jones Parrish.* Ms. Parrish operated a school where she instructed students in typing and shorthand.
- *Mabel B. Little.* Ms. Little operated and owned the Little Rose Beauty Salon to meet residents' haircare needs.

The community stake of these individuals and many more accelerated the economic growth of the district, benefiting its citizens.

Best Practices: Connecting the Past and the Present

Although ultimately, additional measures will need to be employed to address the impact that systemic racism has on Black people's participation in systems of ownership, business owners can and should engage in strategies that foster ownership and increase wealth-building opportunities. In formulating approaches to address economic development, leaders must think creatively like O. W. Gurley, who did not seek to merely start a business but build an empire that encompassed the entirety of the community.

- *Encourage Black business startups.* Black Wall Street developed systems that assisted new businesses. In the present and into the near future, existing Black-owned businesses must take responsibility for encouraging and cultivating startups through mentoring and other programs to help entrepreneurs plant, nourish, and grow their businesses.
- *Support existing Black businesses.* It bears repeating that supporting Black businesses is vital to Black communities for the individual and public benefits they generate, including helping to close the racial wealth gap, strengthening economies, and creating jobs.[17]

CONCLUSION

As we look back at the community that was "Black Wall Street," the people's accomplishments are a source of pride and a testament to their creativity and inherent greatness. In reflecting on their achievements, it can also seem that we are far removed from the circumstances that propelled them to action. Or are we merely on a different day with similar struggles? The urgency of their day presented challenges with issues that we now take for granted. Yet as current realities and statistics demonstrate, despite many advances since the establishment of Black Wall Street and the carnage attendant to its destruction, Black people are *still* confronted with persistent challenges that impede their progress.

It is in view of these acknowledgments and a desire to edify Black communities that we find value in looking to the past to gain insight into the future. The principles highlighted in this book—access to resources, collaboration, education, health care, communication, and ownership—are elements that are interlocked and interdependent. Successfully integrating them into strategies for improving Black businesses and Black communities will require participation from various entities, both human (multiracial and multiethnic) and organizational, private businesses, and state and federal agencies.

The account of Black Wall Street in this book has not focused on the appalling incidents that led to the extermination of this community, Many of the citizens of Greenwood were prosperous; all of them were Black. On May 30, 1921, White terrorists killed hundreds of its residents and burned the town to the ground, a civilian air patrol raining down bombs. The historical record lists a large quantity and variety of such incidents of Whites destroying Black wealth.

As the nation is having a dialogue about inequities and systemic racism—the current buzz phrase being "diversity, equity, and inclusion"—we must continue to hold the difficult conversations and take the bold steps that lead to change at the *core* of our economic and social systems, not just on its margins. And in remembering and venerating the pioneers of Black Wall Street, we envision and build New Black Wall Streets in America's Black communities.

Imagine what the future for those businesses in the Greenwood District might have looked like if they persisted to the present day. Perhaps they would have been comparable to this contemporary list of US retail and restaurant companies founded in the 1800s:[18]

- 1818—Brooks Brothers
- 1826—Lord & Taylor
- 1858—Macy's
- 1859—The Great Atlantic & Pacific Tea Company
- 1861—Bloomingdales
- 1867—Saks Fifth Avenue
- 1865—Carters
- 1866—Mobil
- 1866—Sherwin-Williams
- 1870—Exxon (Standard Oil)
- 1873—Barnes & Noble
- 1876—AT&T
- 1876—Chevron
- 1878—Foot Locker
- 1881—Target
- 1883—The Kroger Co.
- 1892—Abercrombie & Fitch
- 1892—Shell

LaRachelle Samuel-Smith, PhD
and William H. Turner, PhD

Unfortunately, we will never know. What we know for sure is the shared principles of the Greenwood founders built a thriving community of economic prosperity. Over time new communities will be built by reimagining the future, combining the lessons from Black Wall Street business founders and the examples of their White counterparts that succeeded throughout history.

SOURCES

1   https://www.jec.senate.gov/public/_cache/files/ccf4dbe2-810a-44f8-b3e7-14f7e5143ba6/economic-state-of-black-america-2020.pdf.

2   https://www.history.com/news/black-wall-street-tulsa-race-massacre.

3   Lessons from Black Wall Street - 1.pdf.

4   https://www.forbes.com/sites/antoinegara/2020/06/18/the-bezos-of-black-wall-street-tulsa-race-riots-1921/?sh=42807f31f321.

5   https://www.oxfordlearnersdictionaries.com/us/definition/english/resource_1#:~:text=/%CB%88ri%CB%90s%C9%94%CB%90rs/%2C,especially%20to%20increase%20their%20wealth.

6   https://www.mckinsey.com/industries/public-and-social-sector/our-insights/the-economic-impact-of-closing-the-racial-wealth-gap?cid=soc-web.

7   https://www.marketwatch.com/story/heres-why-black-families-have-struggled-for-decades-to-gain-wealth-2019-02-28.

8   https://www.nytimes.com/2020/07/15/business/paycheck-protection-program-bias.html.

9   https://www.biblegateway.com/passage/?search=luke+12%3A48&version=NKJV.

10 https://www.uschamber.com/on-demand/diversity-and-inclusion/legacy-of-tulsas-black-wall-street.

11 https://www.forbes.com/sites/rhettbuttle/2020/06/09/
black-business-must-be-part-of-solution-conversation-with-
ron-busby/?sh=714ab51a4f90.

12 https://www.fels.upenn.edu/recap/posts/1071#:~:text=
When%20not%2Dfor%2Dprofit%20hospitals,support
%20their%20own%20workforce%20needs.

13 https://leadersinternational.org/focus-areas/communication-
for-economic-development/.

14 https://gateway.okhistory.org/explore/collections/TULSA/.

15 https://www.nielsen.com/us/en/insights/article/2015/black-
influence-goes-mainstream-in-the-us/.

16 https://www.cnn.com/2021/05/16/success/black-wall-
street-trnd/index.html.

17 https://www.greenamerica.org/blog/6-reasons-support-
black-owned-businesses.

18 https://www.liveabout.com/oldest-us-retail-companies-
2891902.

ABOUT THE AUTHORS

LaRachelle Samuel-Smith, PhD, cofounder of the Table SALT Group—which consults with small businesses and organizations offering tools, tips, and resources for growth and leadership development—is an educator dedicated to researching entrepreneurship in underserved communities and the progress of historically Black universities in the Southern land-grant educational system.

William H. Turner, PhD, author of the critically acclaimed memoir *Harlan Renaissance: Stories of Black Life in Appalachian Coal*, retired as distinguished professor of Appalachian studies and regional ambassador from Berea College. Dr. Turner also worked as a research associate with Alex Haley on the production of *Roots* and serves as coauthor of *Black to the Future*.